# CONTENTS

# SCHOOLS

1900 | 1915 | 1930 | 1945

BOYS

1900
school-leaving
age – 12

1918
school-leaving
age – 14

'Twelve years old? Time to finish with that school and get out and find yourself a job!'

You'd be surprised if your mother or father said this to you on your twelfth birthday, but parents did say it in 1900. Since then, people's ideas about education have changed enormously. The time line above shows some of the changes since 1900. In the rest of this

1960

1975

today

GIRLS

1947
school-leaving
age – 15

1972
school-leaving
age – 16

book you can see what these changes meant for children at school.

The information comes from photographs, official documents, letters that schoolchildren wrote at the time and people's memories of their schooldays.

Asking people about their memories is one of the most important ways of finding out about school life earlier this century.

You can add to the information in this book by asking your parents and grandparents what they remember.

# A SCHOOLDAY IN 1900

Imagine sitting in a classroom in 1900. Look at the desks. The seats and tops are joined together and bolted to the floor. You will sit in your desk for an hour and a half until break. Look around the room, at the pictures on the walls. Can you see out of the windows? If you were in the back row, would that fire keep you warm? From the way this classroom is set out, can you guess how you are expected to behave during lessons?

## THE TIMETABLE

Here is your timetable for Monday. Lunch-time lasts two hours because there are no school dinners and some children go home for a meal.

| | |
|---|---|
| 9.00 Bible Reading | 2.00 Drawing |
| 9.40 Arithmetic | 2.40 History |
| 10.30 Break | 3.20 Break |
| 10.40 Geography | 3.30 Drill |
| 11.20 Dictation | 4.00 Writing |
| 12.00 Lunch | 4.30 Home |

These boys are doing the *drill* listed in the timetable. ▶

## THE LESSONS

You spend a lot of time learning things by heart. For example, in history the teacher expects you to learn the names of all the kings and queens of England in order, starting with Ethelwolf.
In geography, you learn the names of the capes, bays, mountains and rivers in Britain.

A classroom in 1900 ▼

You have a handwriting lesson every day. The younger children draw letters with their fingers in trays sprinkled with sand. Older children write on slates with squeaky pencils also made of slate. Slates are used because they can be wiped clean. At the age of nine, children use steel-nibbed pens. The nibs are dipped into inkwells so that pupils can practise their writing in copybooks. Biros were not invented until 1947.

*Stephen usherped the crown. This prince was famed for his persernal faleur and died a naturel death. Richard 1st met his death by an arrow, from a crossbow as he was besieging the castle of one of his vassel's to wrest from him a treasure.*

These are some of the answers a girl in Leeds wrote for her history test. It looks as though she has learnt her work but doesn't quite understand what she is writing. Her spelling isn't very good either!

In 1899 all children had to stay at school until they were 12 years old. Many of their parents would have left school at the age of ten. More education meant that children could get better jobs than their parents, as it says in the song below, which was sung in music halls in 1900.

*There, he's off! the young varmint, he's needled;*
*whenever I talks about work*
*He puts on his cap and he hooks it;*
*he's a notion he'll go for a clerk.*
*The green-stuff ain't up to his 'ighness; he don't like*
*to serve at the stall;*
*He fancies hisself in a orfice, a fillin' o' books with his scrawl.*

A: Why did the shortcake sing?
B: Because it saw abundance.

# PRIZES AND PUNISHMENTS

During the 'no-cane' strikes in 1911 children visited other schools to persuade them to go on strike too. Here a newspaper photographer chats to two policemen while they keep an eye on the boys. ▶

In the first half of this century children were caned for talking, for getting ink blots on their work, for laziness or for making mistakes. Boys were caned much more often than girls – girls were often kept in at lunchtimes.

Arthur Burley was at an Elementary School near Truro in 1920 and he remembers the cane well.

*You're bloody right it hurt. The teacher had these bamboos as big as your finger and about three foot long and when you hold your hand out and the stick come down you'd think he's nearly cut your fingers off. When you'd 'ad the first one you'd nearly jump off the floor. Well, time you'd 'ad two on each hand, for about an hour you were rubbing your hands because they was that painful you had a job to write afterwards.*

As more teachers were properly trained and classes became smaller, the cane was used less often. By the 1950s some schools only caned boys when they were acting dangerously. At Hampton School in Leeds, for example, boys were caned for getting on or off moving trains and running out of the school gates into the road. The cane was abolished by law in 1987.

## STRIKES

With so much punishment it wasn't surprising that some schoolchildren rebelled. In 1911 schoolboys in Llanelli started a strike against the cane. Over the next two weeks there were strikes in many parts of Britain, including Aberdeen, London, Glasgow and Hull. Most strikes only lasted a few hours, but in Dundee thousands of children were out of school for weeks.

▲ Children believed that if you put a hair on your palm the cane would break. After a caning, orange peel was rubbed on the sore palm to take away the sting.

## PRIZES

As well as punishments there were rewards and prizes. These were often given for good behaviour. Playing truant from school was a problem at the beginning of the century so there were special prizes for children who never missed a day's school. At the end of the year there was a grand prize-giving ceremony. Some schools still have this ceremony. Children who do well in different subjects or who work especially hard are given beautifully decorated certificates or books.

A: What did the monkey say
as he cut off his tail?
B: It won't be long now.

◀ Alice Spencer was a good student. She won certificates for religious knowledge three years running.

9

# SECONDARY SCHOOLS

Mr Scott was born in 1902. He remembers when it was time for him to take the entrance exam for *Grammar School*.
His teacher said 'You've got a chance of passing, but I know it wouldn't be any use you going in for it. Your parents could never afford to dress you up to the standard required of all the gentry boys when they go to Grammar School.'

▲ William Brown was a popular fictional character in the 1920s and 1930s. In the picture above, notice his patterned socks and cap. These showed that he went to Grammar School.

## GRAMMAR SCHOOLS
Most Grammar School children were what Mr Scott's teacher called 'gentry'. Their parents paid school fees and they didn't take the entrance exam. A quarter of the places were kept for poor, clever *Elementary School* children like Mr Scott. The local education authority would have paid his fees but not for his uniform or books. So he stayed at Elementary School another year and went to work at thirteen.

Very few – one in fifty – Elementary children went to Grammar School. Some went to *Central Schools* where they learnt a trade or office skills. They stayed until they were sixteen. Most stayed on at their Elementary School until they were old enough to go to work.

## THE ELEVEN PLUS
Mr Scott went to school before the first world war. It was only after the second world war that there were enough secondary schools for everyone.
All children took a test called the *Eleven Plus* when they were ready to leave junior school. Those with the highest marks went either to Grammar School (all places were free by then), or to *Technical Grammar Schools* if they wanted to be technicians. The rest went to *Secondary Modern Schools*. They studied craft and office work as well as ordinary school subjects.

A: Close your eyes and spell ICE without the E
B: I C
A: No, you can't with your eyes shut.

◀ At Central School, you went on with ordinary school subjects and learnt a trade or office skills as well. These girls in 1935 are showing the pictures and records used in teaching French.

Jane    John    Sandra    James    Susan

## COMPREHENSIVE SCHOOLS

From 1950 there were other changes. People began to think that ten or eleven was too early to decide a child's future. Some parts of the country had more Grammar School places than others – Merioneth in Wales had places for 60% of the children, whereas Nottinghamshire only had places for 14%. Obviously this wasn't fair. Gradually the three kinds of schools became one: a *Comprehensive*, where all children could go and where all subjects were taught.

| The Earliest Age You Could Leave School | | | |
|---|---|---|---|
| 1888 | 1918 | 1947 | 1972 |
| 12 years | 14 years | 15 years | 16 years |

**Jane Smith**
Born 1900   Left Elementary School at thirteen and went to work as a housemaid.

**John Smith**
Born 1920   Left Elementary School at eleven and went to a Central School. He learnt carpentry and went to work at fifteen.

**Susan Smith**
Born 1940   Passed the Eleven Plus and went to a Grammar School until eighteen, then to university and became a doctor.

**James Smith**
Born 1940   Failed the Eleven Plus, went to a Secondary Modern until fifteen, then to a Technical College to train as a plumber.

**Sandra Smith**
Born 1960   Went to a Comprehensive School at eleven, then to Teachers' Training College at eighteen.

# PLAYGROUND GAMES

These are some of the games schoolchildren have played this century. Have you played any of them? Your parents and grandparents might remember some of these games. Perhaps you call them by different names.

*Chimneypots* is like leapfrog except that when you jump you have to put something on the 'frog's' back. If you knock anything off you become the 'frog'. In *Honeypots* the shopkeeper and customer test the pots to see if they are good. They swing each pot three times, singing, 'Is she rotten, is she sound? Is she worth a million pound? Toss her up and toss her down. She is worth a million pound.' If the pot's hands unclasp she is rotten and therefore out.

The skipping game is called *Birthdays*. The rope-turners chant the names of the months and the skippers come in on

their birthday month. *Fivestones* really uses six stones. You throw one in the air, pick up one of the stones on the ground and catch the one you have thrown before it lands. Next round pick up the stones two at a time. In *Sevens* you throw the ball against the wall, first seven times, then six and so on. Each time throw it a different way: between your legs, turning round before catching it.

In *May I?* the caller tells each person what kind of step to take. Some of the steps are: banana step – slide one foot as far forward as you can; cup and saucer – one bob jump, one with feet wide apart; buckets – step through linked hands; lotus – go down on your knees and take a 'step'; scissors – jump feet apart, then together. The first to reach the caller takes his or her place.

In *'Peas and Beans'* the walls are 'home'. When the catcher calls 'Peas and Beans' everyone runs to another wall. Anyone caught helps the catcher.

# PRIVATE SCHOOLS

## CHANGES

After 1900 the government offered to help the Private Schools with money if they would take some free pupils in return. Some schools became part of the state system. Others now have part of their costs paid and take some free students. Some have remained completely independent.

## PROGRESSIVE SCHOOLS

Most Independent Schools taught in a way similar to State Schools. Some, called progressive schools, believed that arts, crafts and music were as important to children as academic subjects. They also thought that children learned better if they were encouraged to find out for themselves instead of expecting teachers to give them all the answers.

Some schools gave children the responsibility of planning their own work programmes. They also set up school councils where children could have a say in how their schools were run.

Some of these ideas sound quite normal now but they were thought very unusual in the 1920s.

Do you attend a *Private* or a *State School*? Most people go to State Schools.
A Private, or Independent School is one which is not run by the government. Only 7% of all children go to Private Schools.

In 1900 there were many types of Private Schools in Britain. There were charity schools for poor children, and also fee-paying schools started by people who hoped to make a profit out of them. There were some *Public Schools* which had been set up before to teach poor children alongside fee-paying students. By 1900 all Public School students paid fees. There were also schools run by church religious groups for their own children.

◀ The Small School in Devon started in 1982 with nine pupils. It is run by parents and teachers together. Local people, like this basket-weaver, come in to help with lessons.

The Jews' Free School began in 1732. Now the local education authority pays for everything except for special lessons in Hebrew. Children do not pay to attend the school. ▶

## STARTING A SCHOOL

Would you like to start your own Independent School? You can. The only rule is that your school must be checked by a government inspector. She or he can close it down if they think it is not good enough.

Not all Independent Schools are as old as Winchester College, which began in 1382. Nant-Y-Cwm School in Wales was started by a group of parents in 1977. They wanted a school for their children which followed the ideas of a philosopher called Rudolf Steiner. So, they bought an old schoolhouse and paid for the furniture and a teacher by holding fairs and barn dances.

A: What would Neptune say if the sea dried up?
B: I haven't a notion.

▲ At this independent junior school, children are expected to organise their own private study.

# PHYSICAL EDUCATION

There was little equipment – no gyms – and nowhere to play games. Before the first world war there were very few playing fields or swimming baths. It was not until 1933 that teachers were encouraged to spend part of the P.E. lesson playing games for fun.

## MEMORIES

Even after the second world war, in many schools P.E. was less fun than it is today. One girl remembers her lessons in 1950.

*The whole summer term, every lesson, we practised our routine for the school display. When the great day came all our parents were invited and the whole school, all eight hundred of us, lined up on the playing field. For half an hour we all bent and stretched and waved our arms, trying to keep in time with the music on the loudspeakers. I was terrified in case I made a mistake. Imagine, seven*

If you think that the children doing drill on this page look as if they are in the army, you would almost be right. Games in 1900 were for lunch-times and after school. Drill was not meant to be fun. It was meant to make you fit, to teach you to stand up straight and to obey orders quickly. Many of the exercises were based on the training given to young soldiers. Many of the first drill teachers had been in the army themselves.

*hundred and ninety-nine girls all bending one*
*way and me the other – with my parents*
*watching!*

## FOOTBALL

Although the boys in the picture opposite
are practising in their asphalt
playground, they are wearing football kit
and will go to the local park for inter-
school matches. Bill Woods remembers
how in 1916, when he was in the school
football team, the teacher would give
him a football shirt for matches. But on
his feet he wore an old pair of army
boots. . .

*With a hole in the bottom and a big toe cap an'*
*I used to be able to kick the ball the length of the*
*pitch in dry weather.*

## PLAYING FIELDS

In 1936 the Education Department told
all local education authorities that did
not have playing fields that they must
provide them.

▲ Boys playing football in the
1930s.

By the 1950s dance was being
taught in all girls' Secondary
Schools as part of the P.E.
lesson. In this photograph, taken
in 1987, a professional dancer
has come into school with his
company to work with the pupils. ▼

A: Why did the cowslip?
B: Because it saw the
bulrush

◀ Girls doing drill in 1906.

# THE EVACUEES

Would you like to leave your parents and go with your schoolfriends and teachers to live with a strange family for three or four years? When the war began in 1939 the Government thought the big cities would be bombed. So, instead of going back to their own schools in September, nearly a million children were sent to foster-families in towns and villages in the country. These children were called *evacuees*.

One of the ways in which historians collect information is by asking people about their memories. The second world war made a big change in people's lives. Everyone who was at school then will remember something – perhaps the air raid warning going in the middle of the lesson, using slates to save paper, the evacuees arriving, or even being evacuated themselves.

## LIVING IN THE COUNTRY

Country-living was a big change for the evacuees. Many had never been out of a city before. One girl later wrote:

*I could not settle to village life, the unfamiliar accents, the country quiet.*

Another boy remembered:

*For us 'vaccies' there was no welcome from the local kids. All they extended to us was a fast-moving fist between the eyes.*

Although most evacuees missed their parents, many were very happy in their foster homes. One boy later recalled:

*It was another life – fresh country food, a room of my own and the countryside. To me, then, it was a wonderland of fields and farms and animals.*

## POVERTY

You can see that most of the boys in the photograph don't have coats or proper shoes. Some of the poorest evacuees had no pyjamas or even underclothes to take with them. They were not used to sleeping in beds with sheets. As it was

▲ Boys being evacuated.

the end of the summer holidays, and they had not seen the school nurse for weeks, some had lice or fleas.

Many foster parents were shocked. They had never seen children like this before. People began to feel that schools must provide more care for children. In 1944 a new Education Act was passed to improve schools. This provided free dinners for all poor children and free milk and medical treatment for every schoolchild.

## SCHOOLING

The evacuees usually shared the village school with the local children. They often worked in the classrooms in the mornings and outside after lunch. The war didn't stop for school holidays so many children couldn't go home even for Christmas. Most of the men had joined the army so, at weekends, the children helped on the farms.

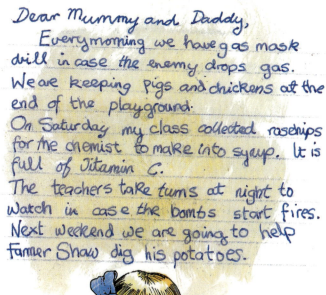

Dear Mummy and Daddy,
Every morning we have gas mask drill in case the enemy drops gas.
We are keeping pigs and chickens at the end of the playground.
On Saturday my class collected rosehips for the chemist to make into syrup. It is full of Vitamin C.
The teachers take turns at night to watch in case the bombs start fires.
Next weekend we are going to help Farmer Shaw dig his potatoes.

◀ Two evacuees helping on a farm in Wales.

A: What did the bull say when it swallowed a bomb?
B: Abominable!

# NEW WAYS OF TEACHING

'What do you think?'
If you were at school in 1900 you would probably never hear your teacher ask this question. Teachers had lists of what their pupils were supposed to know. Their job was to make sure that everyone learnt the same thing. In drawing lessons everyone drew the same vase. In reading lessons everyone read the same stories.

This was partly because many teachers did not know a great deal themselves. Some had just left school. They taught during the day and went to teaching classes in the evenings. There was very little equipment in schools so there was not much variety in the lessons.

All these things began to change slowly. After 1903 no one was allowed to teach until they reached the age of sixteen. In 1925 pupils who wanted to be teachers had to stay at school until they were eighteen and then go to training college for two years.

One of the most important changes came in a report written by the Department of Education in 1931. It said that teachers in primary schools should allow children to have their own ideas and find out things for themselves, instead of always being told everything.

## EQUIPMENT
The only equipment a child at Elementary School needed in 1910 was a slate, a slate pencil and an abacus to count with. Most schools had a stone built into the wall beside the front door to sharpen slate pencils on. During the second world war many schools went back to using slates to save paper.

▲ The equipment a child needed at Elementary School.

◀ Boys in a science lesson in 1911.

Children doing an experiment in 1987. ▼

After the second world war the government gave schools more money. This meant there was enough equipment in science lessons for children to try their own experiments instead of always watching the teacher.

The photograph above shows a science lesson in 1911; the equipment belongs to the school. The teacher knows exactly what is going to happen because he has taught this lesson many times before. In the photograph opposite, taken in 1987, the children have built some of the equipment themselves. They are experimenting. They have set themselves a problem and are working out how to solve it. The teacher will help them if they ask, but otherwise she will not tell them what to do.

The first schools' radio and television broadcasts (1924 and 1957) gave new ideas to teachers all over the country. More variety in lessons made learning much more interesting.

A: Twenty copycats by a river.
   One dived in.
   How many were left?
B: Nineteen?
A: None – all the rest copied.

# CO-EDUCATION

Should boys and girls learn the same things at school? Should they work together? Nowadays we think this is quite normal but it was not always so. In the middle of the nineteenth century almost all schools were Private. They were either for boys or for girls, never both. People believed that boys and girls needed to learn different things.

## LEARNING TO BE LADIES
In 1858 an angry father took his daughter away from her Private School because he didn't like what she was learning. He told the headmistress 'If the girls were going to be bankers, it would be very well to teach them arithmetic as you do, but really there is no need.' He thought, like most parents, that the only skills a girl needed were music, dancing, drawing and French. Before 1850 that was all most girls' schools taught.

## SCIENCE AND MATHEMATICS
A few women didn't agree. They believed that girls were just as clever as boys and that they should be taught science and mathematics. They set up Private Schools for girls which proved that girls could do as well as boys. More and more parents began to want their daughters to have the same kind of education as their sons.

The girls in the photograph below are at a Private School and are probably seventeen, although they look older because of their hairstyles and clothes. This school, Cheltenham Ladies' College, was one of the first girls' schools to have microscopes.

◀ A Botany lesson at Cheltenham Ladies' College.

Not many schools allowed boys to learn cookery. This photograph was taken in 1942. In 1975 it became the law that boys and girls could learn all subjects. ▶

◄ Girls practising laundry skills.

A: What has four legs and yellow feathers?
B: Two canaries

## CO-EDUCATION

In state Elementary Schools in 1900 boys and girls were taught the same subjects, except that girls had extra lessons in housework and babycare. In the photograph above, the blackboard tells you what these Elementary schoolgirls are doing. The curtains are mended before being washed. The girls on the left are mixing starch to make the cotton lace nice and crisp – there were no nylon nets. They are ironing with Flat irons which have to be heated up on the stove.

In most schools boys and girls went into the school through separate doors and they sat in separate classrooms. When it was time for Secondary School, people thought that they should go to different schools. They were afraid that if they sat together they would think about each other instead of working.

There was a problem though. There were more Secondary Schools for boys so fewer girls had the chance to go on studying. In 1944 a law was passed which resulted in there being enough Secondary Schools for everyone. People's ideas changed too. More people began to think that it was wiser for girls and boys to be educated together.

# HEALTH

If you and your friends were at school in 1904 instead of now, how would you be different? First, you would all look two years younger than you do now because you would be 10 cm shorter and weigh 10 kg less. Nearly all of you would have holes in your teeth and some of you would have earache. A quarter of you would find it hard to see the blackboard because you would not have the glasses you need. Half the girls would be itchy with headlice because of their long hair.

▲ In 1927 over a thousand children died of a disease called diphtheria. After the Second World War, the government encouraged parents to have their children immunized against diphtheria. The government used pictures, such as the one above, to show that the children would not suffer any ill-effects from inoculation.

◀ The school nurse inspected boys for cleanliness before they saw the doctor. Some schools built bathrooms so that children could bath before lessons.

Girls caught headlice more easily because of their long hair. If the nurse found lice or ringworm she would send the child home. ▶

24

## ILL HEALTH

How do we know this? Until the Boer War in 1899, no one really knew how unhealthy people were. However, when men tried to join the army, many were found to be unfit. Therefore the government asked teams of experts to find out why.

Some of the experts studied schoolchildren. They found that at one school in Bradford a quarter of the children had worn the same clothes day and night for over six months. Some schools only had buckets for lavatories. Children cleaned their slates by spitting on them and rubbing them with their sleeves. One in three children in Edinburgh did not get enough to eat. No wonder so many children were sickly.

## THE SCHOOL DOCTOR

In 1907 a law was passed for school doctors to examine every schoolchild. At first parents had to pay for treatment but later it was free.

Some local authorities began to serve hot dinners – not in school but in local church halls. They were free for the very poorest children.

There were new lessons too: P.E. and games instead of drill, and lessons about healthy eating. There were also lessons about the use of toothbrushes.

School Dinners 1918
3d (1¼p) per meal
Mon:    Lentil Soup, Rice Pudding
Tues:   Pea Soup, Jam Pudding
Wed:    Suet Pudding, Rice Pudding
Thurs:  Lentil Soup, Potatoes, Suet Dumpling
Fri:    Vegetable Pie, Cornflour Pudding

What is missing from this menu? How hungry would you have to be to enjoy it?

# CHILDREN WITH SPECIAL NEEDS

## POSSUMS AND OPTICONS

Because of the new electronic aids, many children with disabilities can now go to mainstream schools.

John is blind. He does the same lessons as the sighted children in his class. He has a braille typewriter, a cassette recorder to take notes and a calculator which speaks the numbers as he presses the keys. His Opticon can 'read' the printed words in ordinary books. It translates the letters into small rods on a special plate. John reads the rods with his fingers.

David has some lessons at his special school and some at the mainstream school next door. He is in a wheelchair and cannot use his hands. He has a special typewriter called a 'possum' which he works by tapping out a code with his feet on two pedals.

The photograph below shows school ambulances in 1908 bringing children for their day's lessons. The photograph was probably taken because the school was quite new. Before 1893 there were only a few special schools, for blind and deaf children, which were run by charities. During the first twenty years of this century, state schools were built for children with disabilities. They went to day school until they were thirteen and then to boarding school to learn a trade so that they could earn their own livings.

In 1908 deaf children learnt basket-making, woodwork and tailoring so that they could earn a living. ◀

◀ School ambulances in 1908.

'When I first went to the ordinary school I wasn't sure how the other children would accept me. Naturally at first they were curious, but when they got to know me better they seemed to accept me. They open the doors for me and help me in different ways, but they talk to me as though I wasn't handicapped.'

A rhyme to say to cowards:
Canty canty custard
Ate a pound of mustard
Burned his tongue and home did run
Canty canty custard

▲ This miniature electric typewriter can be plugged into an electric wheelchair. Children who cannot speak can type messages wherever they go.

# SCHOOLS WITH A DIFFERENCE

Do you know what you want to be when you grow up? Even if you do, you'll probably wait until you've left school and then start training. Some children find that they have a special talent when they are very young. These children can go to schools where they fit their ordinary school subjects around their training.

Other children find it difficult to go to ordinary schools because they are travelling around the country. Their school comes to them. The 1944 Education Act said that all children must be educated, but didn't say they had to go out to school. Even today, some children are educated at home by their parents.

▲ Canal Boat children.

Some of the schools below are very old, some are quite new, some have closed because they are no longer needed. They show how education is always changing to meet children's needs.

## THE ITALIA CONTI THEATRE SCHOOL

The children at this school spend part of every day studying acting, singing and dancing. This theatre school was started by the actress Italia Conti in 1911. She was training some child actors and when the play they were in finished, their parents asked her to go on teaching them. Children have to prove that they have talent before they are accepted here. Some pay for themselves; others have grants from their local education authority.

◀ The Italia Conti School.

Children from Gerry Cottle's circus in their 'school' van. ▶

## CANAL BOAT CHILDREN

In 1900 there were hundreds of families living on canal boats carrying goods from one town to another. Councils set up schools at the main stopping places so that the children could have some lessons. Sometimes, for example at Sutton Stop, north of Coventry, parents dropped their children off and they lived at the school for a week or two, going back on board when their parents returned south. The canal boat schools are all closed now.

## CIRCUS CHILDREN

The children below, are from Gerry Cottle's circus and are at school. Their classroom is a van which travels with them. This means that they do not have to go away to boarding school or start a new school every time the circus moves. They also have plenty of time to help in the circus and practise their juggling and riding after school. Their travelling school started in 1980.

## WELLS CATHEDRAL SCHOOL

The first mention of a cathedral school at Wells was in 909 AD. Now the school is a large co-educational school. Most of the children follow an ordinary school course but some come to the school because they are talented at music. Their timetable is arranged so that they can practise for three hours a day. There are also sixteen boys who belong to the cathedral choir. They practise for an hour every morning besides singing in the cathedral every evening.

Wells Cathedral School children. ▶

# THE STORY OF ONE SCHOOL

## WATFORD FIELD SCHOOL

Everything on these two pages is part of the history of one school. From the outside it looks almost the same as in 1891, but inside everything has changed.

At first girls and boys were taught in separate parts of the school. Every child had to pass a test every year to go into the next class. The attendance officer came every week to see who was missing. (When the circus came to town lots of children played truant.) There was a prize of a silver watch for every child who didn't miss a single day's school.

A silver watch was often awarded for good attendance. ▶

## MEMORIES

These are some of the things that people who went to the school before 1920 remember:

*Every morning we sang the same hymn. There were very few textbooks and no homework. . . no radio or television. . . no school outings except to the open air swimming pool down by the river — that was cold! No school buses, no school dinners — we took a sandwich and a bottle of cold tea for dinner. . . no fêtes or open days. . . and the loos were outside across the playground.*

Below are some of the things that have happened at Watford Field since 1891. Does your school have a similar history?

| 1891 | The school opens. |
|------|-------------------|
| 1914 | The first woman teacher joins the boys' school. |
| 1915 | The children go swimming for the first time. |
| 1926 | The football team wins the inter-school competition – half day holiday for the whole school. |
| 1929 | The school changes into a junior school and everyone leaves at eleven to go to secondary school. |
| 1930 | School milk provided for the first time. |
| 1939 | No one is allowed to school without a gas mask. |
| 1941 | The first school dinner is served. |
| 1970 | Inside toilets are built. |

▲ The classroom in 1917.

## THE CLASSROOM

The photograph above was taken in 1917. The girls look stern because they had to sit very still for the camera. They are in their best pinafores and are showing off their sewing and knitting. Can you see anyone wearing spectacles? The girls with short hair have been ill and had their hair cut to keep them cool. Each row of desks is on a higher platform than the one in front so that all the children can see the teacher.

▲ This is the same room today. You can still see the tiles on the walls but the platforms have gone. What else has changed?

Every school had to keep a diary where the head teacher wrote down everything important that happened. Reading this is a good way of finding out what school life was like.

## THE SCHOOL LOG 1900

Jan 9th   All boys from Watford Union to be excluded from school for a few days as one of their number has fallen with scarlet fever.

Jan 11th   This day I returned to the clerk the form relating to the Fuller Scholarships with only one name entered thereon.

Jan 15th   Mr Bristow [an attendance officer] paid his weekly visit this morning.

Jan 16th   This morning I received notice by postcard that the Labour Certificate Examination would be held on Saturday 27th at the Victoria Boys' School.

# GLOSSARY AND INDEX

*Central School* a type of secondary school which taught office and trade skills. After the second world war these schools became Secondary Modern Schools

*Comprehensive School* a school which takes all children at eleven without an entrance examination

*co-education* where girls and boys are taught together

*dictation* an exercise where the teacher reads out from a book and the children write what she reads to practise their spelling and punctuation

*drill* the first type of P.E. given to children. It was based on army training

*diphtheria* an infectious disease of the throat

*Elementary School* a state school for children aged 4 to 12 years old. These schools became primary schools after the second world war

*Eleven Plus* a test in English, arithmetic and intelligence which all the children after the second world war sat, at the age of eleven, to decide which kind of secondary school they should go to

*evacuees* the name given to children who were sent out of the big cities during the second world war to keep them safe from bombing

*Grammar School* In 1900 you had to pay to go to Grammar School unless you passed an examination and the local education authority paid your fees. After the second world war most Grammar Schools were taken over by local education authorities and became free. You had to pass the Eleven Plus to go there

*Local Education Authority* part of the County Council that looks after schools

*Private/Independent School* a school which does not get any money from the government and the parents pay school fees. A few children at these schools have part of their fees paid by the government

*Public School* a private school which used to take some students free

*Secondary Modern School* after the second world war the Central Schools became Secondary Modern Schools. Children who failed the Eleven Plus exam went there. At first children did not take exams. Later they took the CSE examination

*Special School* a school for children who might for various reasons find it difficult to cope at a mainstream school

*State School* a school paid for and run by the government and local education authorities

*Technical Grammar School* a school set up after the second world war for children who passed the Eleven Plus but not well enough to go to Grammar School. They specialized in engineering and technical subjects